I0236457

All rights reserved
Copyright © Crispin, 2025

The right of Crispin to be identified as the author of this
work has been asserted in accordance with Section 78
of the Copyright, Designs and Patents Act 1988

The book cover is copyright to Crispin

This book is published by
Grosvenor House Publishing Ltd
Link House
140 The Broadway, Tolworth, Surrey, KT6 7HT.
www.grosvenorhousepublishing.co.uk

This book is sold subject to the conditions that it shall not, by way of
trade or otherwise, be lent, resold, hired out or otherwise circulated
without the author's or publisher's prior consent in any form of
binding or cover other than that in which it is published and
without a similar condition including this condition being
imposed on the subsequent purchaser.

This book is a work of fiction. Any resemblance to
people or events, past or present, is purely coincidental.

A CIP record for this book
is available from the British Library

ISBN 978-1-83615-212-5

Poeticus Pictoralis III

Joy, Sadness & In-between

A small form of daffodil named "Poet's narcissi"
and a style of painting that enhances
the beauty of the subject

This third and probably final book of poetry
is dedicated to Andrew & Sue Baldwin
in the continued memory
of their wonderful daughter... Kate...

By
Crispin

With original art purchased in fields and
emporia for relatively small amounts of money
and the occasional painting by Angie and
caveman level daub by me.

**Grosvenor House
Publishing Limited**

Colourful Quotes

His shape spoke of youth, so handsome in
truth, no time yet to swell, by eating too well,

A caress from the fingers of the sun,
a touch for the many, given by the one,

And built a breach of hedge to broach the field,

And so, I watch a mother, stroke her
daughter's head,
No hair, just little feathers. No hand, a beak
instead,

If a harp was placed before me, I would weave
that gentle sound,
and their tears would dry, like summer sky
when June is all around,

Arrows of tiny Sparrows,
wing and swerve through the narrows,

Canopies of Cowslips cast shadows on the
grass and sway with gentle whispers as the
breeze attempts to pass,

Reds that with a whiplash crack
make Shakespeare curse his words for what
they lack,

Brown river, brown bank, brown leaves,
brown stick thrown, brown dog retrieves,

For this is the language we understand,
we careless, hairless monkeys of the land,

Rivers too small to be given a name,
rage through the gutters with only one aim,

Eyes have turned from forward, to peering
back, for what's been done looks better...
Sun-riser beats Sun-setter,

Dirt-track dust, loose-planked huts, orange long-boned yawning mutts,

His black eyes... roll over white, in the slash of the kill, the moment of bite,

Broken, rotten stumps of trees, show nature's comfort with disease,

When birds, like Phoenix, burn across the sky and fish are cooked in briny cauldron...
Please don't ask me why?

For the carbon we emit in our little daily lives, has made the odds quite slim, that planet earth survives,

But, just as summer flies upon our dreams, winter's cold can also pass with speed, or so it seems,

The pendula motion of the needle that swings, suggests a rigidity to all living things,

The distance belying how hard they are trying,
for all that's serene, is not closely seen,

It's easy to mistake a junior Rook for a Crow;
it's called a "Rookie error" for those who didn't
know,

To find a fajita cast aside, by someone with too
much tequila inside,

One should not shrink and curl, as a leaf
exposed to heat. One should stand foursquare
and plant one's solid feet.

Dark green moss and lichen of pastel hue, wrap
the precious host in blanket warm.

Whilst in the bramble wigwams, feathers fly,
on little wings, on little things, whizzing by.

Looking on, a pure white swan sits in
judgement of everyone...

Index of contents

Poems of Joy

Jet-black foal

The jet-black foal, was the colour of coal,
He was a shock to my senses, beyond the wire
fences,
He walked over on stilts, his head slightly tilts,
Even that young, raised in mud and in dung,
He was alert to the man in the shirt,
Whose staring was rude, but who might have
some food...

My eyes could not quite trace, the features of
his face,
All was black...
He walked like a model, a curve in his back,
His shape spoke of youth, so handsome in
truth,
No time yet to swell, by eating too well,
He was fresh from the caste, perfect youth
cannot last,
At this second in time, his silhouette is sublime,
Without a discernible feature... a truly
magnificent creature.

Blue Tit's dream

They used to steal our milk you know,
well… not our milk… Our cream,
Peck through the foil and in beak go,
It was a Blue tit's dream,
Burnt match feet grip the rim,
And every single ounce of him,
Would tongue and suck and lick,
For "top of the milk" was very thick,
Back when it was delivered,
When "Slipper-shod" women often shivered,
As on their winter doorstep standing,
Reaching down and cold blue-handing,
They'd pick their "Pinta" up,
And curse the little bird who'd dared to sup…

Oil on board painting by Rex Flood.

New page each day

Each day, those of us who live, are granted,
An episode of fixed duration… planted,
A page, upon which to write,
Our story, our glory, things of dark to bright,
Every day, an opportunity new,
To throw off the dull repeating pain, which only
    grew,
By being given far too many pages,
By being tolerated like tantrums and rages,
So now… today… a brand new book is writ,
And from page one, is full of humour and of
    pithy wit,
Crammed so full of observation kind and dry,
It cannot fail to bring a tear, to moisten human
    eye,
For freedom to be better, will only come,
From the hand that holds the pen between the
    fingers and the thumb.

Our Fatsia Japonica

Around our birdbath we let a Fatsia grow,
It started beneath the bowl, it started below,
And over the years, we have seen it rise,
Until now, when the washing birds are
    obscured from our eyes,
Seven-fingered palms of leaves, achieve
    a curious angle,
Bitter black-berries, the evil bunches,
    grape-like dangle,
But animals will eat them, at a push,
If there's nothing for the sweeter beak,
    on any nearby bush,
And in December, white cauliflower heads
    appear,
Flowers which attract the insects, to drink the
    heady beer,
Wasps and Bees and Flies, none of them will
    sneeze,
At the pollen message carried, upon the winter
    breeze,
It's good to know that Bees, who started
    on the G of bang!
Could have a place to feed... as the hidden
    Robin bathed and sang.

Blackberry heatwave

The blackberry is early, this summer 22,
Bluish-black and heavy, long before it's
    due,
Heavy with water, not fallen from the sky,
But, sucked up from underground, ground
    so parched and dry,
Upon the thorny arm, where the ripe
    ones sit,
There are smaller "on their way ones," red
    or pink, tight-knit,
Smaller still, the green ones, fruit in
    embryo,
Also flower centres there... they let their
    petals go,
All four stages, at this moment can be seen,
Upon the heatwave bramble-arms, with
    leaves of dusty green...

The stile

The stile, although man-made, fits the scene,
The silvered grainy wood has always been,
One wouldn't know that man had pulled his
    saw,
Through un-seasoned plank, when it was raw,
And built a breach of hedge... to broach the
    field,
The locking of a gate, ensures the land is
    sealed,
So ramblers can enter and can leave,
And walk the lanes and woods and freely
    breathe.

Holding hands

When lovers destined to be,
Are holding hands like you and me,
The blackbird's and the robin's singing,
Like angels to the heavens winging,
Sweetening even the sweetest fruit,
The harp is plucked, as is the lute,
Bees are busier,
Butterflies are dizzier,
And all the lighter land,
When you and I are hand in hand...

The old man

The old man lay dying, his wife sat by his side,
He rolled his head her way... and looked at
  her one-eyed,
He said, "You gave me thirty wonderful years,"
She smiled at him and gently through her
  tears,
She said, "We've been together fifty years...
  How can you forget?"
And as he died... he replied... "The thirty
  before we met..."

Gift of care

Only through a selfless love,
Is self-interest able to be surpassed...
Who would have thought that it could be so?
That by giving all, one could be left with more,
As an empty heart is heavy,
So will a full heart be light,
For understanding breeds empathy,
And empathy is the gift of care.

Feathers & Beak

Today I saw two black birds sitting on the
  muscled bough,
Of the gnarled and knotted oak, just off the
  road, that's busy now,
They were never blackbirds... as Crows they
  were designed,
Side by side they sat and faced away... I am
  behind,
And so, I watch a Mother... stroke her
  daughter's head,
No hair, just little feathers. No hand, a beak
  instead,
Straightening her little blouse and tucking
  shirt-tail in,
The mother showed that human-traits are
  DNA within,
The mother flew off to another tree,
The youngster watched her fly away and then
  looked down at me,
And flew as the crow flies, a straight-line to
  her Mum,
Mum had known, when risk was seen, her
  child would surely come.

The Oaks of Magna road

On Magna road, near the stone-carved pillars,
Of Canford school and associated villas,
There stand the denizens of our land,
Not pupils or masters, whose tenure spanned,
Only decades of self-important issues,
I talk of denizens constructed of much
   longer-lasting tissues,
The Oaks of Magna road...
were standing there before a king, signed
   the Baron's code,
If half a dozen men of six feet tall,
Were to face the trunk and reach around it all,
They may just fail to form a human ring,
That's the scale of magnitude of this living
   thing,
Boughs so large that they themselves are
   trunks,
Passing liquid through them, like unabated
   drunks,
In spring, today, their leaves are light green
   youth,
A single year to hang then fall, a sacrifice
   to truth,
A thousand times the acorn harvest spread,
And maybe one will find, within the soil a
   long-term bed,
And be allowed to grow to massive scale,
To see the next millennium... before it too
   will fail.

Oil on board... Signed Diana M Jones 1974.

Arrest the fleeing hour

It's easy to imagine that the white hydrangea's
   head,
Is not a ball of petals, but butterflies
   instead,
Frozen in a cluster, as if the clock has
   stopped,
And now the rangy beauty, with living
   creatures topped...
Has all it ever wanted and has halted
   time's advance,
You'd think that they were petals, if you
   gave a casual glance,
The timeless plant has unsuspected power...
The ability to stop the clock... and arrest
   the fleeing hour.

Music

If I could play piano, my fingers would type
    a tune,
And those who heard would cry because...
    they think it ends too soon,
If a harp was placed before me, I would
    weave that gentle sound,
And their tears would dry, like summer sky
    when June is all around,
If my mouth embraced a trumpet's kiss,
Heaven's choir... could only hope... to sound
    a bit like this,
And if my fingertips could brush a guitar's
    wires,
The rhythm would encapsulate all mankind's
    desires,
A drum would soon succumb and time beats
    out,
The throbbing heart of music's soul... leaves
    nobody in doubt,
That music feeds the spirit and raises up
    the mind,
To a place that screens and movie scenes
    can very rarely find.

Nature's pleasure

One day alive is a treasure,
Using death or nothing as a suitable
     measure,
Against which, one may compare,
The sun and the breeze and the warmth
     in the air,
Jasmine's travelling scent,
Leaving all in a daze, wherever it went,
Heavy bumble-bees,
Clamber in the petals with yellow velvet
     knees,
Arrows of tiny sparrows,
Wing and swerve through the narrows,
Of the limbs and branches of the slumbering
     trees,
If one is lucky, one knows and one sees,
That each day alive is one's treasure,
One resides on this side, by the grace of
     nature's pleasure.

From the jetty at Peveril point, Swanage

Groaning planks, slapping waves, clinking
    chains,
Screaming gull, flapping sail, fish remains,
Seaweed stink, salty spray, tight-skinned face,
ebbing tide, mussel clumps, open space,
Fishing boats, orange float, tangled line,
Lobster pots, slimy kelp, smell of brine,
Little cottage, wispy smoke, tiny town,
Empty boathouse, concrete slipway, sloping
    down,
Sitting silent, nose inhaling, nothing thinking,
Simple beauty, simple duty, inward drinking...

Oil on board... Signature illegible...

The root of the problem

Turnip rustling gangs put the law to the test,
Down in the rural heartland of England's deep
    south-west,
The clang of forks and spades, can commonly
    be found,
At night-time in the turnip fields, as they dig
    the hardened ground,
Pirates of the root-veg, gangsters of the field,
A lookout on the gateway, his eyes are
    always peeled,
The ethos of the criminals, is fear and power
    and dread,
The controller of the turnip game, is dubbed
    the "turnip-head,"
The turnip-head is ruthless and it's he,
    who sets the price,
Of the turnips that the addicts crave, to
    satisfy their vice,
Some will have it powder-dried and sniff it
    through a straw,
Others boil and mash it… they claim that,
    that is what it's for,
Heavy lies the crown upon the turnip-head,
For challengers are manifold and they,
    all wish him dead,
He worked his way from "Carrot-boy," up the
    villain's ladder,
But, every time his power grew, it only made
    him sadder,

Now he plans how he'll escape and leave the
    gang behind,
Yet every time that he gets close, he has to
    change his mind,
For he is trapped by all the deeds that got
    him to the top,
So much so that he may never now, find a
    way to stop…

Objet dieu

Look at this clay, look at this sand,
All that's required is the genius hand,
Of Emile Galle or Rene Lalique,
To mould or to etch 'til an item unique,
Comes into being from the ground we have
    trod,
From the fabric of the universe, to an object
    of god.

Murmuration at dusk

Dusk is quietly settling to the west,
Behind me to the east, night's conquest...
is completed,
And the day for another night has been
    defeated,
But, I look west...
West is where the Starlings resist their
    nightly rest,
And rise in numbers, I cannot count,
Shifting, stretching, shrinking... inestimable
    amount,
Darker is their cloud, when their shapeless
    mantle shrinks,
Only to stretch and lighten, see the sun,
    it sinks,
They wheel and swerve, to squeeze the final
    drops of day,
Then as a single thought, they put themselves
    away.

Watercolour and ink on paper by Angie.

Crispin and Angie

Four decades and a half have passed,
    yes its' 45 years later,
And if I feared that love can't last,
    "au contraire," it's even greater,
For what we now possess, between us,
Is knowledge that I'm no Hercules and you
    my love no Venus,
But, strip away the unfocussed aspirations
    of the young,
And sing together life's sweet song, the way
    it should be sung,
Then what remains of love, is the concentrated
    essence,
Of love's true light, which cannot be, surpassed
    in luminescence.

Seven-spot Ladybird
(Coccinella Septempunctata)

Why is it that we love you little ladybird?
Why is the black-spotted red one, the beetle
    most preferred?
Well… you went to all the trouble, of putting
    on that dress,
It makes you more acceptable, I feel I must
    confess,
You are not funereal or scurrying to hide,
You are very welcome, to come and be inside,
A quantity well-known and useful in the fight,
To keep the roses clean of aphid, fly or mite,
You hide from cold in winter, from freezing air
    attack,
In spring you will emerge from every door and
    window crack,
You'll sit upon my finger, a colourful delight,
And thrill, but disappoint me as you split in
    gentle flight.

Wagtail encounter

Just beyond the 18th hole... I sat on a grassy
    mound,
Adding up the strokes we'd taken on our
    golfing round,
Mike was standing, as he joked, he may not
    get back up,
We laughed at that, but there's some truth
    in age's bitter cup,
Our mood was good... we'd both played well,
We'd drawn the match and had tales to tell,
Of drives that hung in the sky forever,
Of pitches and chips and putts, so clever,
As if to share our great rapport,
The tiniest Wagtail you ever saw,
Hopped up to us... and as if in greeting,
Inclined his head, cheerfully tweeting,
We talked to him as we would a child,
Friendly words, in tone so mild,
The long straight feathers of his tail,
His soft round chest of yellow pale,
His black needle beak, his tiny stature,
Yet he knew, we were not... animal catcher,
So, now with total freedom found,
One flicker of wing, he left the ground,
And landed on my trolley's wheel,

A needle jab, a wriggling meal,
He held it in his beak like pliers,
The standard tool of all the fliers,
As if to show us, why he risked it,
Showed the cheek, that took the biscuit,
A few more twitters, as if in thanking,
And away he hopped, across the banking,
That surrounds the green on the final hole,
God bless that Wagtail, god bless his soul...

Tears, smiles and thoughts

I will sell you a bucket of tears,
A bucket of tears, gathered over the years,
All of the worries, that then became fears,
Garnered in droplets in a bucket of tears,

I will buy a bag full of smiles,
A bag full of smiles, gathered over a while,
All of the laughter, that giddies and beguiles,
Captured quite easily in a bag full of smiles,

I will cherish my mind full of thoughts,
A mind full of thoughts, of all kinds and sorts,
All of the knowing, that loving has brought,
Has given me insight that cannot be bought...

Beats flying

I am a sea-bird, not a tree-bird, but a
    free bird,
I am in the sky, often high, open eye,
I am searching for a fish, my only wish,
    a tasty dish,
I spot a silver flash... make a dash,
    then a splash,
I am underwater... I have sought her,
    now I've caught her,
I clamp my yellow beak around the
    silver body sleek,
I rise once more into the air, my food
    is wriggling... I don't care,
I turn the fish to face my gullet, it could be
    Bass... it could be Mullet,
I force the meal down, before the fish has
    time to drown,
I am feeling hunger-sated, satisfied, almost
    elated,
I spy an empty rowing boat, unattended, still
    afloat,
I circle down and perch upon the bow, happy
    now,
I rest and I am grateful I'm not trying...
I rest upon the prow... It sure beats flying.

My pitiful effort.

The world is round... but flat

Said the Squirrel, from atop his tree...
"Our world is definitely round!"
"Yes... but flat!" Said the Ant, from his place
    upon the ground,
"There are many other worlds than your
    roundabout," said the Bee,
"Yes... across the black-ground," said Squirrel,
    coming down his tree,
"I guess we are just lucky that it's not shaped
    like a fruit,"
"Or we would just go flying off"... said Owl,
    with a hoot.

You Squirrels

You squirrels liven up our garden,
Resident alien, no need for pardon,
You leap with agile ease,
As you travel through your path of trees,
I see you as a friend,
As upside down, you suspend,
Like a cat… you're long,
When hanging like a dinner gong,
Dexterous with feet and hands,
You've come to us from distant lands,
But, grey is all I've known,
And red ones like to be alone,
On islands or up north,
Towards the bridge o'er Firth of forth,
They can have the ruddy squirrel,
Those that live up round the Wirral,
And I will keep my southern grey,
My favourite squirrel any day!

Our England

My England is clothed in greens and greys and
    browns,
All the rainbow flowers flow across the fields
    and towns,
Yellows that would shame the Spanish sun,
Blues of all the hues, sweetly down the
    valleys run,
Reds, that with a whiplash crack,
Make Shakespeare curse his words, for what
    they lack,
Purples echo the flowing gown of priest,
Ample falling water will promote the very
    least,
To flash its beauty light,
So, England can continue to win the fight
    for right,
And be the land where every colour wins,
For England can be proud, of every shade,
    of all her skins…

Grassy bank

A little grassy bank, wears a hedge as its
    crown,
And flower heads like sweets, upon the dark
    green tumble down,
The Dandelion head, is an explosion of the
    sun,
And will compete, with the neat and pretty
    Daisy one,
Buttercups are willing, to reveal with a tickle,
Those who like their dairy and whom with
    lover's sickle,
Will take the glossy yellow beauty from its
    stem of life,
To gently graze the under-chin of potential
    future wife,
Forget-me-nots are fairy spots of a blue so
    light and bright,
That to forget it would be tantamount to total
    loss of sight,
Like tiny children dancing in little lacy
    dresses,
The beauty of the innocence Forget-me-not
    possesses,
Canopies of Cowslips cast shadows on the
    grass,
And sway with gentle whispers as the breeze
    attempts to pass.

Kingfisher day

I labour on the upslope of the heavy iron
    bridge,
My muddy boots afford the grip, to make it to
    the ridge,
The apex of the arch of girders planned,
To permanently guarantee, the river's always
    Spanned,
Brown river, brown bank, brown leaves,
Brown stick thrown, brown dog retrieves,
I double take…Vivid blue! Petrol iridescent
    too!
Flash above the water!
Splash! No camera could have caught her,
Blue of silver shimmer!
Consummate as flyer! Consummate as
    swimmer!
Orange flag, as under-wing exposed,
To slow you as you reach the bank, beak is
    not quite closed,
A tiny struggling fish, needs aligning,
Blue again, returns to branch… Kingfisher!
Day defining…

Sunshine

I sit in the sun and I bask,
What more than this, could I possibly ask?
A kiss from the celestial light,
The heat from the passion is browning my
   white,
A caress from the fingers of the sun,
A touch for the many, given by the one,
Is it Love...?
A cloud crossed the face, in the sky up above,
No. It's duty...
But, that won't diminish the feeling of beauty,
For warmth and light are the gifts most
   essential,
And the soul of mankind should be solar
   deferential...

Oil on canvas... Signature illegible.

With us

Little arrows in the snow,
Show us where the Robins go,
With us through the winter,
When water turns to ice and splinter,
With us when the howling wind,
Has all the flailing plant-life pinned,
Still here when the mid-march sun,
Fools us in to thinking, that summer has
    begun,
When courtyard wall excludes the brittle
    breeze,
We sitting with our trousers, rolled up to
    our knees,
Baring skin that's not been seen, for this
    half-year that's passed,
The loyal Robin's colours are nailed firmly to
    our mast.

We are not alone

In my recent experiment, the following
    was found,
That in the observable universe, there is
    known to be around,
A million times, one thousand million times,
    one thousand million suns,
You can call it one quadrillion, but colloquially
    it's "tons,"
So far, one sun has had its system explored
    for signs of life,
The answer found, "on the ground," cuts
    through doubt, like it's a knife,
In a test of one, our very own sun has set
    the proportionate tone,
I estimate… that at this date, its one
    quadrillion to one we're alone.
1,000,000,000,000,000,000,000,000 : 1

Pink Roses

The white that brings us purity and the
    red that brings the fire, collaborate to a
    colour state which could be pure desire,
Pink is what I talk of, pink that's seen as
    weak, but those who share that point of
    view, know not of what they speak.
Pink like Tourmaline, pink like lips, pink like
    roses atop their thorny whips,
On the table, in the Lapis vase, I hope
    your sweet pink roses are as beautiful
    as ours.

Painting is oil on board and unsigned.

Poems of Sadness

The Glories of Man

Into the blue of the skies above Kent,
Out of the blue I'm a pilot just sent,
There's a Rolls Royce at the front of my crate,
But, luxury flying will just have to wait,
For me to survive, a wizard must act,
I'll call upon Merlin, if we are attacked,
For I am to kill any young German men,
Who've flown to the call at eight years past
    ten...
The skies above Kent are a privilege to me,
as is our land, as is our sea,
So, I'll fight with the vigour of the hero I am
and surrender my life to the glories of man...

Oil on board... not signed.

Coco in retirement

I see Coco standing solid, in the distance,
Deep in thought, braced and steeled, a
    half ton of resistance,
Stubborn... still, as if his memory retains,
A time of pulling heavy plough, muscle and
    sinew strains,
A rising cloak of steam through hot wet hair,
Turning quickly back to water, in the cold
    mid-winter's air,
Walking the row from furrow's start to end,
Turning and leaning forward... once more with
    labour's bend,
On occasion to feel the farmer's whip,
If even for a moment, his effort were to dip,
Though Coco has long ago retired... even
    now,
His body through his memory... still wears
    the heavy plough.

Servants of the planet

Agents of the air assemble,
Beat your feathered wings and make us
   tremble,
Occupants of the deepest water,
Rise to the surface and threaten slaughter,
For this is the language we understand,
We careless, hairless monkeys of the land,
Armoured insects form a line,
Climb upon each other's backs and make a
   sign,
For we are blind to danger,
Until we ourselves become the poor and
   starving stranger,
We, of all the creatures, can aspire to God-like
   grace,
As servants of the planet, custodians of this
   place.

Back O' the Wight

The "Barque Auguste" was on the rocks just
    south of the Isle of Wight, in the final year
    of Victoria's reign, it was a fearful, dreadful
    night,

She'd come from Western Australia, from
    Freemantle she had hailed, bringing wood
    to pave the London streets, but ill-fortune
    had prevailed,

A night in the rigging for the crew for fear
    the ship would sink, but the courage
    of the "Atherfield men" saved them
    from "the drink,"

The local lifeboat hauled its way through the
    heavy breakers and saved the stricken
    sailors from the journey to meet their
    makers.

No sooner had the final man (the captain) left
    the ship, than the backbone of the "Barque
    Auguste" began to tear and rip,

A monumental sadness settles on those folk
    who know... what it's like to see a ship
    destroyed... what it's like to see her go.

Acrylic on board signed by Chasper Wait 1982.

Last post

For what did I die? What **did** my death
    yield?
Still cold do I lay… in a far foreign field,
The days you enjoy with the freedom to
    see,
The country I died for… but not saved for
    me,
Look again, look through **my** eyes,
At the fields full of yellow, rolling out to
    sunrise,
The sun that comes up, over an England
    unfettered,
That no other country has **ever** yet
    bettered,
Tell me it's special to see what you see,
My beautiful England, so precious… and
    free,
Raise please, your glass… and give me a
    toast,
As for you, life goes on… beyond the last
    post.

Hard rain

The rain slips over the terrain and down the
    drain,
It lashes… makes dots and dashes… on my
    window pane,
The invisible wind is exposed… the rain has
    that power,
Blown to an angle, this hard-falling
    shower,
Filling the crevices… refuge of the tiny
    sticks,
Of Spiders and woodlice, of ants and of
    ticks,
They scuttle in fear of the water blown in,
To the crack in the wall of the steps by
    the bin,
Rivers too small to be given a name,
Rage through the gutters with only one aim,
To find the path of least resistance,
To shorten the time, diminish the distance,
To where the water all must flow,
The deepest point… the lowest low,
And fill those places… make those lakes,
Then find the sea… for all our sakes.

Hidden Monk

You cannot see me hidden in the shadow
    cast upon the window's arch,
Shadow formed by sun that bathes those
    free of life within a hairy shirt and starch,
I became a monk, that I could feel the
    closeness of our lord,
Fifty years of contemplation and now I find
    I'm bored,
Within my fellow monks I see all the human
    flaws,
Which I had sought to guard against behind
    the great oak doors,
Of this tree-lined, high-walled retreat from all
    desire, except the wish to serve a power
    which we regard as higher.
The higher power, I've come to see, is all the
    best in you and them and me,
I've learned to be a gardener and best maker
    of the mead and as I look now from tower
    high,
I wish my younger self, had thought more
    of selfish need.

Oil on canvas un-signed.

Coconut & Velvet are dead

Both Coconut and Velvet are dead,
The aged pair are grazing now, a heavenly
    field instead,
No longer to depend upon the kindness of a
    stranger,
No longer now unstable diet and diabetes
    danger,
For these were horses left in field to fend,
Upon the tender mercy of unknowns they
    did depend,
No shelter did they have, bar the canopy
    of the oak,
And no hard ground to dry their hooves, when
field with rain did soak,
My single apple every day, my way of showing
    love,
I taught them both, to wait their turn and not
    to push and shove,
The RSPCA would come from time to time
    to check,
That they were not in too much pain and
    pat a sturdy neck,
I loved those horses dearly, stubborn,
    moody, real,
And now I walk to empty field, but empty
    I don't feel,
As blowing in the wind I hear, their voices
    calling still,
And having talked with them for years...
    I guess I always will.

Old

The rooms we must inhabit for the passage
   that we tread,
the narrowing dimming corridor, of which little
   must be said,
The thumbed and dog-eared pages of the book,
that once was fresh and beautiful, gets not a
   second look,
Eyes have turned from forward, to peering
back…For what's been done looks better,
Sun-riser beats Sun-setter,
And there's only so much time, one can attack,
The old must be the brave with stoic trudge,
For long-life's gift, can't be rewarded, with a
   bitter grudge,
Fading eyes, will not be hurt, by the fading of
   the light,
The broken body must depart, for the soul to
   take its flight…

Harry Skinner picks the wires & tells...
the blue-grass story

Simple tales of deep regrets, tangled in the
    crawfish nets,
Dirt-track dust, loose planked huts, orange
    long-boned yawning mutts,
Un-shod leathery shuffling feet, padding to
    the guitar's beat,
Dungarees and week-old meat,
Blue-grass tells the story...

The psychopath shark

All sharks must continually swim,
Or the water unmoved, will suffocate him,
All sharks must continually eat,
Craving the proteins found in all meat,
His mouth, surrounded by teeth,
Is the crown of this predator, all others
  beneath,
It is said, he kills without pity,
A heartless loner, the ocean his city,
His black eyes… roll over white,
In the slash of the kill, the moment of bite,
I pity the psychopath shark,
The absence of feeling, the presence of dark,
The cold of the sea… like the cold in his soul,
Darkens his viewpoint to the colour of coal…

The untouched field

The giant green horse-chestnut tree,
Points upward... whence those horses be,
That used to keep the grasses short,
With constant grazing, blow and snort,
I now see how their diet looked,
Dock-leaves and nettles, all uncooked,
Dandelions, rye-grass and clover,
Things that look like tea-plants... buttercups
    all over,
Broken, rotten stumps of trees,
Show nature's comfort with disease,
As rotten oak... to its knees has come,
Rampant tips of wheat-like grass... surpass its
    hollowed drum,
Once, times past... when wind rushed o'er the
    field,
Tail and mane would flick and fly and yield,
But now, when zephyrs wish to pass,
No sentient is present, just the rippling in
    the grass.

A Devonshire harbour

Pastel pinks and greens and blues,
are the quayside cottage hues,

Cottages now owned by folk
from wealthy cities, there's the joke,

Seldom present, that's the truth,
forcing out the local youth,

For property of such potential,
commands a price that's exponential,

The local young then have to leave... more's
    the pity,
to service the machinery of the wealthy city.

Oil on board... Signed Lambert 1974.

The mole

I found a dead mole on the path by the
    pond,
I tickled his flank, but he didn't respond,
His body was chunky, with silky black fur,
Shiny and healthy, I wished that he were...
His mouth was tucked under his conical
    nose,
Shark-like in style, but not one of those,
His feet at the rear were tiny and pink,
But, up at the head-end, for digging I think,
Were great big hands, each resembled a
    spade,
I pondered the miles of tunnels they'd made,
I bagged up his body and took it to Mum,
She loves all of the creatures, god's souls
    every one,
I wanted to show her a mole in the flesh,
This one was dead, but at least he was fresh,
Sad at his parting, amazed by his design,
We both agreed that his body we'd consign,
Words of commendation to his maker gently
    spoken,
In the soil he loved so much, we laid his body
    broken.

The pain of loss

In the gutter, by the pavement, on the road,
There was a flutter and a wave and nature
    showed,
The indifference, that in our minds we shun,
A Magpie adult pecking at a chick, a tiny one,
A parent of the baby, a little blue tit,
Was running at the killer, hopeless cause, they
    both knew it,
But, instinct overcame the small bird's fear,
Let's call it love, it's brave and it's sincere,
Two weeks later, in the garden at the rear,
I heard three Magpies fighting with screeching
    anger, fear,
In the gutter, by the terrace, on the lawn,
A sleeping, murdered Magpie chick... the pain
    of loss may dawn.

Horses in the field

The grassy hill, patchwork quilts of owner's
   field,
The horses fertilize the ground and graze
   the grassy yield,
With switching tail and tossing mane,
They nullify the fly, their summer bane,
Standing side by side, but opposite in
   direction,
Tails flick faces, in hopeless cause of
   insanity's deflection,
Eventually they all will come to see,
That patience in their suffering, is what
   must come to be,
Perfect moments can be found,
When sun beats down and cracks the
   baked-hard ground,
And the wind is blowing hard enough to
   force,
The flies to shelter down amongst the
   flowering spikey gorse,

Occasionally a shining shoe is showed,
As hoof is raised, to rest its quarter load,
Some would think the horse's maths absurd,
But horses know this method, without the
   written word,
Equine wisdom passed by mare to foal,
Means that resting all four legs, is a realistic
   goal,

The "Jet-black foal" is now a horse full-grown,
And really far too beautiful for anyone to
    own,
Surrounded as he is by wire and tape and
    stake,
He should be in the forest, by the clear
    cold-water lake...

Denouement

It's only when one looks toward the setting of
    the Sun,
That one may see the tangled threads, of
    webs the Spider spun,
Between the uprights of the Iron Gate,
Between the curling metal scrolls, designed
    to decorate...
A feeling of decay,
A denouement at the end of day,
The sun sinks in the west,
Now the web invisible... lets conscience
    come to rest.

The marching parade

A truth has come through focus poor,
From dim-lit vision, behind closed door,
To clear definition and pin-sharp view,
A truth for the spirit of me... and you,
All things of worth, things not in vain,
Must occupy part of our brain,
The part that deals with growth and future,
The careful stitch, the healing suture,
The plighting of our sincere troth,
Investment in our children's growth,
The planting of the seeds,
The culling of the strangling weeds,
The painting of a picture for all time,
Going forward like the words within a
    satisfying rhyme,
For forward we must go,
Until the pumping heart, can no longer
    pump the flow,
Of the blood within our veins,
And only final breath remains,
Only then, must the focus fade,
Drop behind the marching parade,
See the elephant's ample rear,
Move slowly on, become unclear,
The sound of trumpets, thumping drums,
Fading now, quietness comes...

Don't ask me why

There are those which fly above us and there
  are those that swim below,
We, on land, are privy to information they
  don't know,
Yet, even armed as we are, with why the world
  is changing,
Reluctance still prevents us from our lifestyle's
  re-arranging,
When birds, like phoenix, burn across the sky,
And fish are cooked in briny cauldron... Please
don't ask me why?
For I will say in no uncertain terms,
that the whole of human-kind has been no
smarter than the worms.

Sombre beauty

There is a sombre beauty about the shore today,
Two Seagulls wheel around the mast,
Shocking white against the Russian grey,
The spumy foam in wind that tries to blast,
Just rocks the little dingy to and fro,
Forgotten rope, the anchor never cast,
Will see the boat succumb to tidal tow...

The sails that are the only colours in the scene,
Will take their tongues of red away,
Like they have never been...

Acrylic on canvas. Signature is undecipherable.

Kick the habit not the habitat
(to be read in the style of Noel Coward)

Regrettably…we've made the world a smoker.
We've trapped her in a bag, I know that it's a
   drag…
But our actions will inevitably choke her.
For the carbon we emit in our little daily lives
has made the odds become quite slim, that
   planet earth survives.
At least in form that will allow mammal-kind
   to breathe
and unless it's our intention
   to trash the place and leave?
We had better give up smoking…
   before the cancer grips.
And prevent the planet putting another
   Ciggy to her lips.
She's given us, all we need, to help her
   kick the habit.
We do not need more evidence…
   no more dissected rabbit to know that
   we are killing her… and she'll kill us in return.
No more delay. Do it now….
Don't make her… make us… burn.

On this timeless side

I must go back! I left them as they cried,
Huddled in their sorrow, around the bed on
    which I died,
They think because my spirit has removed,
That I am gone... as my empty body proved,
That no longer in their presence do I dwell,
But, still I see them... still I see them well,
I'm torn by my emotions... I hate to see their
    tears,
These were my most precious people, in my
    precious years,
How should I send a message to comfort
    their despair?
I could ring a bell, flash a light, blow in
    someone's hair,
I must go back! I left them as they cried,
But, I will wait until they join me, on this
    timeless side...

Poems of In-between

Isosceles the triangular cat

Is that cat triangular? The one over there...
There's none of the round, some of the square,
It's like some squares have been halved,
And from the resulting triangles a cat has been
  carved,
Well... not so much carved, as constructed,
I think the square on the hypotenuse has been
  deducted,
Not equal to the sum of the square of the other
  two sides,
This triangular cat sits in the bushes and hides,
Is a triangular mouse about to scurry past?
Eating a "Toblerone" or "Dairylea" really fast?
If not, the equilateral cat will disappear,
With no sine or cosine that he was ever here!

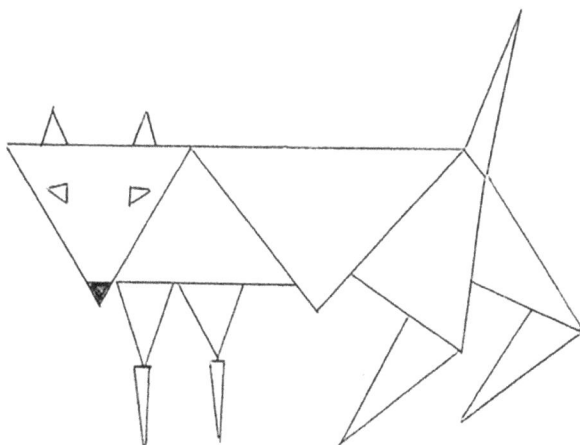

Doodle by Crispin.

Cheeky chunky fly

The chunky black fly just stood still and froze.
Just a second earlier, he'd shot acid from his
    nose.
His intention to digest my lovely sprout...
My intention to deny him... he was getting nowt.

My meal had been delivered with aplomb,
the kitchen now resembled a site upon which
    a bomb,
had blown the pans and pots, into a stack
    beside the sink,
at least, when I am washing up, that's what I
    tend to think.

But, for now all of my energy was engaged
in eating the lovely dinner, only fair I was
    enraged
to see the chunky fly, saying grace,
before, rolling out his nose and sucking sprout
    into his face.

Tempting as it was to slam a fist into my food,
the violence of that action, could be seen as
    rude,

so I flicked my hand dismissively across my
    plate,
telling him to go, in a voice so filled with hate,
that he took off and landed seconds later,
this time his target was, my lovely roast
    Pota-ta.

I waited till he'd finished... had his fill,
the heavy fly rose slowly... I was very still
and as his flight approached my one arm's
    length...
 I swung a heavy backhand with every ounce
    of strength
and sent him like a bullet through the air.

If he lived... he won't come back... he won't...
he wouldn't dare.

First day of winter

A cloud has come to earth… its mist will dull
   our view,

This first day of the winter, extracts its
   tiresome due,

It forces us to wholesome soup,

With coughs and splutters and biting croup,

The smoke before the conjurer, whips the
   cloak away,

Exposing for our shivering bones, the cold
   that's on its way,

But just as summer flies upon our dreams,

Winter's cold can also pass with speed, or so
   it seems,

For Christmas day, is a score and four away,

And on us like a child upon a snowy field at
   play,

Once the festive feast is to the rear,

New Year's Eve and day are quickly here,

And when the final digit of the date falls into
   place,

Then spring will race towards us, with a smile
   upon its face.

Metronomic

The swinging arm of the metronome...click...
   clack,
Stays within the triangular track,
Prescribed by the maker, to guarantee,
That the Click and the clack are a certainty,
Rhythm is used to measure the time,
Sweet like the peach... sour like the lime,
Good like the lord... bad like the devil,
Time is maintained, if kept on the level,
Click... clack,
Time moving forward, never moving back,
The pendula motion of the needle that swings,
Suggests a rigidity to all living things,
For we are governed by the click and the clack,
The heartbeats and moments... inevitably
   stack,
Until the pile has filled to the tip,
The pyramid receptacle... from which we sip,
And we can look forward, to not looking back,
As the metronome swings, click,click,click...
   Clack.

New beak in town

"Get lost! Get out! This ain't your patch,"
Those are the squawks, that I first heard,
"You'll steal our chicks before they hatch!"
"You pirate Gull, you sea-type bird!"
They were not wrong, I am a Gull,
And eggs would be a treat,
I waited for their ire to cool, for there to be
        a lull,
And showed them my webbed feet,
"You'd think from these, that I would be,"
"A bird at home upon the sea,"
"But, truth be known, I cannot stand,"
"The food that's found in sea or sand,"
The Crow and the Magpie, then carked
        at me,
"We are the birds of the land and you are a
        bird of the sea!"
But I replied, with wisdom and flair,
"Surely we are all... just birds of the air."

Painting by E. Gordon Davidge

The un-sifted sand of the path through the
   land,
Holds the purples and greens of the
   breath-taking scenes,
The Verbena and the heather existing
   together,
My spirit is feeding on the scents which
   are bleeding,
Into the air and drifting out there... there
   where the ocean has continuous motion,
There in the vee of the dune, cliffs and sea, is
   a sail pulling hard, like a scene from a card,
The distance belying how hard they are trying,
   for all that's serene, is not closely seen,

Oil on canvas by E. Gordon Davidge.

Raven, Rook and Crow

There are differences between a Raven and a
  Crow,
Not that I believe there are many who would
  know,
But... the Ravens are the larger and less
  social by their nature,
Than the smaller, but just as loud, of the
  Crow-type nomenclature,
The Raven has a bigger beak, which curves
  in swooping hook,
A Crow's beak is straight, but not as pale as
  beak of Rook,
A Rook is like a Crow, but has fluffy feathered
  trousers,
And oily texture, like its gel has come from
  oily bowsers,
It's easy to mistake a junior Rook for a Crow,
It's called a Rookie error for those who didn't know,
The Raven's fluffy feathers are seen around
  its head,
They all, of course are Carrion (known to eat
  the dead),
The family "Corvidae" are the flying undertakers,
Removing all the bodies of the creatures on
  our acres,
Playing well their role as European Vulture,
Clad in black, sombre, as expected by our culture,
They're not the birds that we all love to love,
But, they are not offended... they just choose
  to rise above.

The Stump

It's a stump now, a hollowed bowl,
The bark and harder outer rim remain,
While softer in the middle, rotted to a
    hole,
Shades of green compete for the domain,
Dark green moss and lichen of pastel hue,
Wrap the precious host in blanket warm,
In the sunken bowl, a brackish stew,
Stagnant water, fetid leaves and insects
    swarm,
The bowl is humble and has no thought,
Of what it was, or could have been,
It's lovely still, of its sort,
Organic pond of living green…

Being your Horse

In this Horse's grassy field, that drapes
    across that hill,
I have stood for years now and stand I
    always will,
I am here when you are not,
Still I'm here, when you've forgot,
That in this grassy field,
A doughty friend that will not yield,
Stands and waits the reason for her standing,
Keen to feel the love and stroking tender
    handing,
Wanting hay to fill the iron feeder,
To see and scent the person seen as leader,
In this Horse's grassy field, that drapes
    across that hill,
I'll meadow-graze, all the days, subject to
    your will...

Hot dog

The hot dog sat on the hot stone slab,
A sort of Husky, crossed with a chocolate Lab,
Woolly and white underneath,
On his topside, dark as a thief,
His handsome head is bowed,
He's much too hot, to show he's proud,
He trusts that the door behind his back,
Will not be opened, not even a crack,
As to wear fur in the heat from this sun,
Would imply that he is an eccentric one,
But, nothing is further from true,
Born with the fur, what's a dog gonna do?
But sit in a corner of shade,
And watch all the Mexicans drink lemonade,
Until the sun goes down,
And he can venture into town,
To find a Fajita cast aside,
By someone with too much tequila inside,
These are the moments that he's living for,
as he sits on the step, with his back to the door.

Silver streak

Streak of silver, articulated flesh and muscle,
    scaled,
Through the oceans dark and deep, under seas
    you've sailed,
Darting, snatching living food, as you scythe.
Biting... as you swallow prey alive,
When you can, you join a shoal of fin-friends
    fellow fish,
And so, with safety in the numbers, go just
    where you wish,
Until... surrounded by your foe,
You ball and wheel, a silver cyclone with not a
    place to go,
Dolphins corral you, as Skewers dive-bomb
    from the sky,
The whirling ball of fish sees many die,
When all are sated, the shoal dispersed and
    split,
The silver streak, zips through the depths and
    thinks no more of it.

Oil on canvas... Unsigned... I wouldn't dare.

Is this Mary?

A halo frames this young girl's head.
Her face is simple-pure and her gaze
  lingers.
Unadorned by trappings, pink robe instead
of jewelled gown. Her elongated fingers
are coming together maybe for prayer?
But, for what would she pray?
Has holy calm replaced physical despair
and strengthened her for one more day?

Is it she who has been asked to bear the
  child?
The "king of kings" whose teachings will
  bring peace?
The king with thorny crown, sharp points
  filed...
A painful death upon the cross as his
  release,
if so, she is calm indeed,
filled with God's own power,
building strength for the time of greatest
  need,
the judgement of Jesus, not man's finest
  hour...

1960s Oil on board by James Francis Gill.

It's Christmas Eve

Magic is in the air, it's Christmas Eve.
I kiss my parents, climb the stairs, I still
    believe,
that within this night, a supernatural being,
will visit and reward me, without my seeing.
In such beliefs great comfort can be taken.
In such a world, surely none... can be
    forsaken?
Unless of course, they have not complied,
with all the rules, that keep a child inside,
the bubble of belief.
That magical relief... that all is well in the
    world...

Magic is in the air, it's Christmas Eve.
My children kiss my wife and me, they still
    believe.
My wife has been exhausted by the myriad
    of the tasks.
And I have worked so hard to earn to satisfy
    the asks,
but, still the magic must persist,
for without it, the bubble can't exist
and children must then face the adult truth.
That magic is the perdu, only of the youth
and so, for one more year, the realms'
    preserved and my good girls get all
    the magic
that they know they've deserved...

Judgement of the self

Those of easy mind and fair,
Judge of thyself with due considered care,
Not to dwell on incidents of slight and bite,
Remember context as you should and might,
Apply whatever standard you regard as fit,
For in the end you alone… will be alone with it.

Own your talent

In the humble opinion of this modest poet,
One should own one's achievements... one
    should definitely know it,
One should not shrink and curl, as a leaf
    exposed to heat,
One should stand foursquare and plant one's
    solid feet,
For if, the owner of a gift, bestowed by genes
    and god,
Cannot perceive the talent of the footprints
    to be trod,
Then the full extent of potential... will not
    out,
For confidence, once replaced with doubt,
Will ravage, the creative exhibition bubbling
    within,
And empty vessel critics... will ultimately
    win.

The ditch

Looking from the path atop the hill,
See the grassy field, the air is still,
Tussocks, shocks of unkempt hair,
Punctuate the land, the green, within my
   stare,
The tips of some have turned to straw,
Encouraging the horse to wrench and gnaw,
Whilst in the bramble wigwams, feathers fly,
On little wings, on little things, whizzing by,
The ditch, which can be stream,
Sits still, vibrating in a stagnant dream,
Its glassy surface flicked by flies,
Patient water waits to rise,
Or maybe, to mud it will return?
If the Sun contrives to pierce the cloud and
   burn…

In the sky

Starlings flock and fly in morphing shapeless
   shift.
Tea-leaf dregs, forming, changing, settling
   with the drift,
Kingfisher's flight... speed of light from hidden
   branch to break the water,
Silver fish has no idea of what just came and
   caught her.

A Duck is falling from the sky.
Do not worry... he will not die,
His wings and feet are splayed,
A determined look upon his face...
   he's not afraid,
His body's weight, almost is too great
For his wings to have control,
He lands at speed upon the water...
   and avoids a forward roll.
Looking on, a pure white Swan,
Sits in judgement of everyone...

Overhead, the bird of prey,
Hangs in sky, it seems all day.
This one is a Kite... its red,
A bloody tribute to the dead,
Whose bodies served to sate the
   ravenous mood
of the yawning mouths of the hungry
   brood.

Swallows zip and swerve and pluck the tiny,
Flying insects from the air, with little bodies
  shiny,
When all the family at last is grown, they say
  goodbye,
And sleep in flight, like angels in the clouds,
  high in the sky.

Insular thoughts

I've been here on this desert isle,
This deserted isle for quite a while,
I cast my eyes over my burned red skin,
"Marooned…!" I laugh. "That's what I've bin,"
I pull upon the creeper vine, to raise the
    bamboo cage,
Which I fabricated from materials of just
    sufficient gauge,
To hold together in the choppy sea,
Just below the rocky edge, where I know
    some fish will be,
For bait, I've used the offal of the dead fish
    I had found,
Lying on the hardened sand, just lying on the
    ground,
I put the innards inside my redundant sock,
Held in place within the trap, by a fist-sized
    chunk of rock,
Rock-Salmon, would be wonderful, yes
    Rock-Salmon please,
Maybe find a goat and milk it, maybe make
    some cheese?
I'd heat it up and let it melt and over the fish
    it would run,
I realised then, that my descent into madness…
    had only just Ben Gun,

It's with little jokes like this... with an audience
of me,
That I mitigate my physical trap, with a mind
that still runs free,
Many people feel they're trapped... even in a
city,
Not everyone can free their minds... not
everyone, more's the pity.

Our Lady Notre Dame

Sat we down across from "Notre Dame,"
   awning out and best girl on my arm,
Yellow wine came white with Ice
   and the carafe dripping water,
This "Our Lady" was my wife
   and three carafes I bought her.

We looked upon the beauty of the stone and
   coloured glass
and wondered what, in a thousand years,
   that face had witnessed pass?
For in that time the people of this world
   had learned so much and Jesus
and his miracles, fewer hearts now touch.

The gothic towers and "Midday Rose"
(the window facing south),
Speak more the art of man today,
   with God less in the mouth,
but, fire came five years ago
   and burned "Our Lady" flat,
and the grief was not confined
   to just the French...We all felt that.

The world connected feeling loss at the passing
Of this church,
which took two hundred years to build
    and died in fiery lurch.
As Jesus rose, so has "Notre dame"
    and now the people must ensure
"Our Lady" feels no harm.

Impressionist oil on canvas by
Max Gunther 1957.

Internal dialogue

Whilst talking to one-self is seen as madness,
I view that view with disappointed sadness,
For stability of mind, it is essential,
To converse with the inner self... a voice most
    influential,
The inner voice, is stripped of all pretence,
Devoid of societal taboos, an absence of
    defence,
That voice is the spirit soul, one has within,
Telling truth to your power, without the global
    spin,
The purity of this spirit, a massive strength,
Be true to this inner light...go to any length,
Follow not the herd, if the shepherd is askew,
Act with truth and justice... to your inner voice
    be true.

The glorious pheasant

I pulled my ball left off the tee at the tenth,
It lay out of sight, lousy line, decent length,
As I walked round the corner, it lay there on
    the turf,
In the midst of eight pheasant chicks, all
    pecking at the earth,
Tiny and rounded, clad in feathers of dun,
With no fuss or ceremony, they all acted as
    one,
And filed in a fashion so very calm,
Into a hole in the briar, safely clear from
    harm,
It was then that I noticed... the mother bird
her back was towards me, but I knew that
    she'd heard, she waited and waited till
    she couldn't resist,
Then balled up a claw, like a bony old fist,
And limped in a tired way towards the pond,
Hoping that I, by her act would be conned,
And if my motive was a pheasant to catch,
I would chase after her and not think of her
    batch,
Of children in whom, her love was invested,
In whose defence, her courage was tested,
Cunning and courage... Love has the power
to elevate a pheasant to rise gloriously to
    the hour...

Lord Dog-manly of Cruft

My name is Dog-manly of Cruft.
Long-legged, be-suited not rrrruffed,
The boots are for show,
with their long up-turned toe,
them that don't like it... Get stuffed!
I'm like a dog with two tails in my coat,
my shirt buttons up to my throat.
My trousers are tight,
my hat adds some height.
It's part of a look I promote.
Dog-manly of Cruft is the name.
I put all of the others to shame.
I hope my furry old face
will not look out of place
when I marry that bitch who's a Dame...

A recent photo.

Snotty the Snail

I needed to cross the giant tarmac strip,
ten feet wide that pavement, at least a
   two hour trip.
My home would be upon my back, I didn't
   wish to "Slug it,"
that's when the shell comes off, when it's far
   too far to lug it.
I said goodbye to family as we sometimes
   don't return.
I set my slime to maximum, set my speed
   to "burn."
I inched and stretched and slid and slimed,
as if it was a race for life and I was being
   timed.
I was nearly there now, to the other side,
I could hear my family cheering across the
   tarmac divide.
I turned to wave my eye-stalks in goodbye
   and
suddenly I was lifted by my shell towards an
   eye.
The eye was vast and in a voice that boomed,
an incorrect assumption was incorrectly
   assumed.
I was placed once more back amongst my clan.
Forgive me if I'm not grateful to that interfering
   man,
for sometimes acts of kindness go awry and
   leave a snail like me feeling... dry.

Winter's shadow

Here we are again in the shadow of winter's
   coming,
Strange how strong that shadow, with the sun
   so much subdued,
I strain my ears, but Bees no longer humming,
hide away, with knowledge of the paucity of
   food.
Autumn holds its hand outstretched towards
   my outstretched hand,
but, is moving far away now with the rotation
   of the land.
I shed a tear for all the summertime I didn't
   use. For shorts now abandoned, bare feet
   replaced by shoes.
For all the days I didn't hit the beach, or try
   the sea,
Days I used for other things, or watched too
   much TV.
Golden turns to brown and then to white;
Daytime cruelly shortened, for elongated night,
   but, just as summer whipped and whizzed
   and passed us all.
So the winter's rule will pass and spring will
   come to call.

In-memoriam

Lest the fog of time dim the eye of mind
these words of love and life are given.
So, frail human memory is not alone consigned
to keep the flame alive and heal the riven...

"Crispin. Thanks for being a truly great friend."

My name is Andrew and along with my dear wife Sue, we walk Queen Anne Drive and Magna Road for exercise. If you walk the same route at a similar time on a daily basis, you get to see the same old faces, doing the same old thing, for routine brings comfort.

We spotted a middle-aged man (Crispin) feeding an old wrinkled apple to a pair of un-loved looking horses. I commented to him that the larger of the horses appeared to have a grand white moustache. He laughed and explained some of the background to these two characterful animals. He also mentioned that he was a poet and had written about "Coconut & Velvet" in his soon to be released book of Poetry and art, "Poeticus Pictoralis."

Over the following year, we waved or chatted a few times, until not having seen Crispin for five months, we told him of our sad news… The death of our lovely daughter Kate at the age of Forty-four and how we were trying to be strong for her husband Jamieson and our granddaughter Sophia. We told him of how beautiful the funeral had been and to our surprise Crispin expressed a desire to see the "Order of Service" and to see the images of Kate which were incorporated therein.

Three weeks later, we saw Crispin on the trail and handed him the "Order of Service" and once more to our surprise, from his rucksack Crispin produced his two books of poetry, as he had now released his second book and wished to make a gift of them to us. We read the poems and enjoyed the lovely paintings from his Mother, his wife and his daughters and there was much to comfort us within those pages, for Crispin's books were uplifting and positive in their perspective.

A couple of months passed and we commissioned Crispin to write a poem to commemorate the life of our wonderful Kate. At his request we visited Crispin's home and talked at length about Kate, her personality, her work, her loves and supported this with pictures and details of her friendships. Within 24 hours Crispin had written not one, but two remarkable poems about our special girl. The first, entitled "I was Kate... I made you proud" Crispin explained, was written in a "state of instinct" in ten minutes with no hesitation or amendment (and is our favourite).

I was Kate...
I made you proud

I'm in the peace between the wars,
Divine release from all my chores,
Surrounded by the love from those,
I inherited and those I chose,
Timeless peace suspends my being,
Nothing now prevents my seeing,
That nothing must be seen as failed,
Because duration was curtailed,
For in those years, I loved much more,
Those wonder years... those forty-four,
Not for me the sullen shroud,
I was Kate... I made you proud.

by Crispin

The second poem was "Of Kate..." and according to Crispin was crafted in the manner one might throw a pot or carefully paint a portrait, this incorporated details such as the great honour bestowed upon Kate's memory by her boss Josie and her employer, "Carnival UK", whereby the company's flags outside Carnival House in Southampton, were at half-mast shortly after Kate's passing and references are made to our intention to add photos and butterfly decoration (courtesy of Kate's husband Jamieson) and "sweetly frame" the poems upon our living room wall. References are made to Kate's daughter, seven year-old Sophia's comments as her mother slowly faded, that "she is still beautiful" and she was "Sophia's sleeping beauty."

These poems have given us daily comfort and Crispin's offer to feature this memoriam within his third "Poeticus Pictoralis" book, feels like a legacy of which our beautiful loving daughter Kate... would be proud.

Of Kate...

These words attempt to grasp a person passed,
A gesture of love and respect... Flags at half-mast,
Too great this person Kate to be contained,
Within some rhyming lines, though sweetly framed,
A force of nature, clearly loved by all,
Strong and kind throughout life's rise and fall,
Sea-grey sapphire in her eyes and Sophia in her soul,
Her loving husband Jamieson made this trio whole,

As sister, daughter, mother, wife... she embraced all family duty,
And at the end still beautiful... Sophia's sleeping beauty,
No stranger was Kate to unconditional love,
Dad Andrew, Mum Sue, put no-one else above,
Their daughter and son, Kate and James,
In Kate's lovely life, these were the lovely names,
The size of the loss that Kate's loved-ones now endure,
Is far too huge to explain, of that much I am sure,

If we measure success in how much we achieve,
Then Kate was successful, we have to believe,
The lists were a measure of how to commit,
To tasks and objectives and keeping things fit,
But, what she achieved will always be clear,
Measured by the people, who hold her so dear...
Those people are many, their love running deep,
Kate is alive in the memories they keep.

by Crispin

www.ingramcontent.com/pod-product-compliance
Lightning Source LLC
Chambersburg PA
CBHW040804150426
42813CB00056B/2647

*9 7 8 1 8 3 6 1 5 2 1 2 5 *